春雨惊春清谷天
夏满芒夏暑相连
秋处露秋寒霜降
冬雪雪冬小大寒

本教材为2016年度教育部哲学社会科学研究重大课题攻关项目
“中国书法文化国际传播的理论与实践研究”（16JZD031）阶段性成果

二十四节气

秋

風調雨順

Fall: Season with Timely Breeze and Rain for Crop Raising

The Twenty-four Solar Terms

主编：周斌 周佳楠
Editor-in-chief: ZHOU Bin, ZHOU Jianan
副主编：Roy Ye 尹冬民
Associate Editor: Roy Ye, YIN Dongmin
插图：孙凌雁
Illustrator:SUN Lingyan
书法：盛兰军
Calligraphy: SHENG Lanjun
翻译：江凌
Translators: JIANG Ling
封面题字：Roy Ye
Calligraphy on the cover: Roy Ye

华东师范大学出版社

Nini, I recently noticed that lots of tree leaves were falling. Is it time to start a new solar term again?

You are right, Jerry, it is Beginning of Autumn now. Summer is over, and the season of autumn starts. As the ancient people said, “A falling leaf reveals the arrival of autumn,” which means when tree leaves are falling, it comes to the season of autumn.

妮妮，最近好多树叶都掉了，是不是又要开始新的节气了？

杰瑞，你说得没错啊，现在是立秋了。夏天结束了，秋季开始了。古人说“一叶落知天下秋”，说的就是树叶掉落、秋天到来的意思呢。

二十四节气与十二星座对照图

The table of the Twenty-four Solar Terms and the corresponding astrological signs

Contents

The Symphony of Autumn

目 录

秋季乐章

立秋

Beginning of Autumn

Li Qiu

The story of

Beginning of Autumn

Important facts about Beginning of Autumn

Beginning of Autumn is the first solar term of autumn, which is a herald of autumn. It comes between 7th and 9th August every year. At the time of Beginning of Autumn, the weather has gradually become cool in the morning and evening. There is a big temperature gap between day and night. Autumn is a season of harvest when crops are getting ripe and ready to be reaped.

Changes after Beginning of Autumn

Sunflowers bloom; peaches are ripe for picking.
Cool breeze blows; white dewdrops appear.
Winter cicadas sing softly; crops keep growing.

立秋大事记

立秋是秋季的第一个节气，预示着秋季即将到来，时间点是在每年的8月7～9日之间。立秋时节，早晚逐渐凉爽，昼夜温差变大。秋季是收获的季节，农作物开始成熟、被收割。

立秋变化

葵花开放，桃子成熟。
凉风始至，白露初降。
寒蝉低鸣，庄稼生长。

篆书 (zhuan shu) | Seal script

“立”字的本义是“站立”。篆书“立”的字形像一个人分开两腿，站立在地上。

“立” means “to stand”. The seal script of “立” resembles a man standing straight on the ground with his legs apart.

篆书“秋”字的左半部分像一株成熟的水稻，右半部分像长须长足的蟋蟀。蟋蟀在秋天鸣叫，所以“秋”的本义是指百谷成熟、蟋蟀鸣叫的季节。

Looking at the structure of the seal script of “秋”, we can find that the left part resembles a plant of mature rice, and the right part resembles a field cricket with long antennas and long feet. Field crickets usually chirp in autumn, so the original meaning of “秋” refers to the season when all grains and crops become mature and field crickets start chirping loudly.

跟着杰瑞写一写

Practicing calligraphy with Jerry

楷书（kai shu）| Regular script

在学写"立秋"之前，我们先来学习书法中一些常见的基本笔画。之后大家可以举一反三进行练习。

Before we start writing "立秋", let's learn some fundamental strokes in Chinese calligraphy first. Then you will be able to apply them to your later practice.

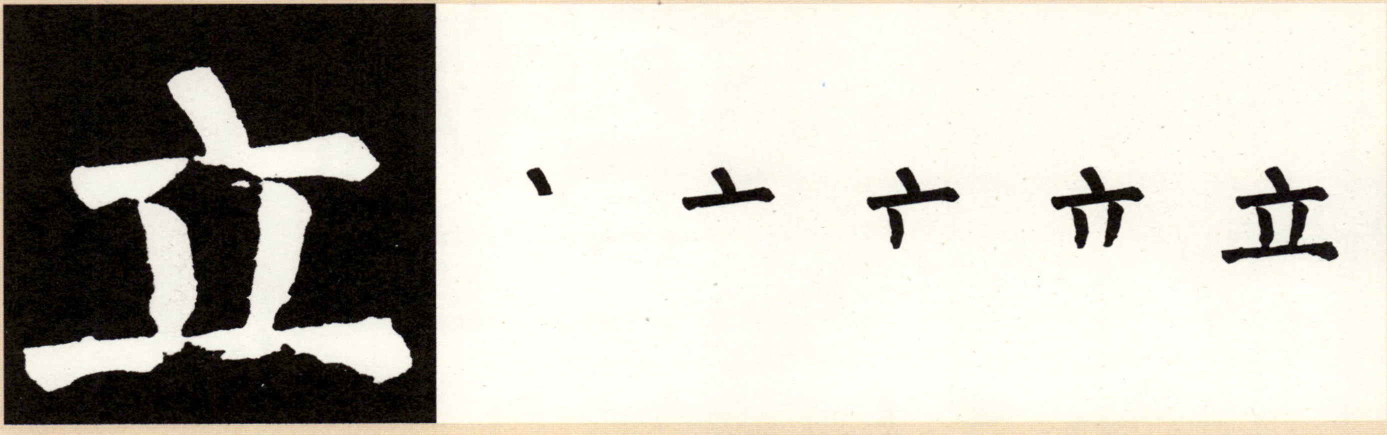

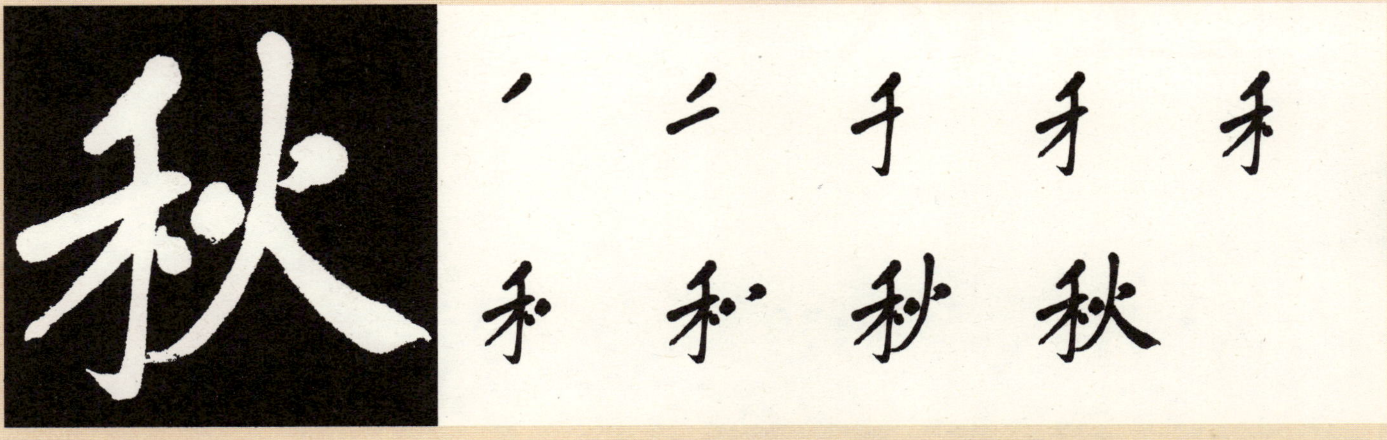

剪一剪、画一画

Paper cutting and graphic design

Make a gift with Chinese characters "立秋"

剪剪画画

做立秋的礼物

跟着妮妮和杰瑞做送给朋友的礼物

Let's make some gifts for our friends with Nini and Jerry

Paper cutting by Nini

妮妮的剪纸

Graphic designed by Jerry

杰瑞的画

猜一猜、说一说

Let's make a guess

Let's make a guess with Nini and Jerry

与妮妮和杰瑞一起猜一猜

与"立秋"对应的是哪个星座？

Which astrological sign corresponds to Beginning of Autumn?

Let's have a competition with Nini and Jerry

与妮妮和杰瑞一起比赛

说出与"秋"有关的词语

Try to say as many words as you can that are relevant to "秋"

处暑

End of Heat
Chu Shu

Important facts about End of Heat

The story of

End of Heat

End of Heat comes between 22nd and 24th August every year. "处" stands for "finish", which indicates that the hot summer is coming to an end. At the time of End of Heat, the weather is getting cooler and cooler. It is rather hot during the daytime, however, there is also a spell of hot weather after Beginning of Autumn, which is called afterheat (the autumn tiger). But it becomes cool and clear on the early morning and at late night. Rain occurs less and it is turning into the climate of autumn.

Changes after End of Heat

Everything withers on the earth; the autumn tiger appears.
Eagles begin birds hunting; seedlings are about to mature.
People are preparing to worship their ancestors.
People appreciate the beautiful moon sight in this enjoyable autumn season.

Tips

The autumn tiger, which refers to a short period of afterheat days, appears at the transition time between summer and autumn.

处暑的故事

处暑大事记

处暑的时间点是在每年的8月22～24日之间。“处”是终止的意思，代表炎热的夏季即将过去。处暑时节，天气逐渐转凉，虽然白天比较炎热，还有“秋老虎”余威，但是清晨和夜晚变得凉爽，降雨渐渐减少，气候逐渐向秋季转变。

处暑变化

天地始肃，秋老虎现。
老鹰捕猎，禾苗将熟。
中元祭祖，迎秋赏景。

小贴士 “秋老虎”：指八、九月交汇间出现的短暂回热的天气。

跟着妮妮学一学
Learning Chinese calligraphy with Nini

篆书 (zhuan shu) | Seal script

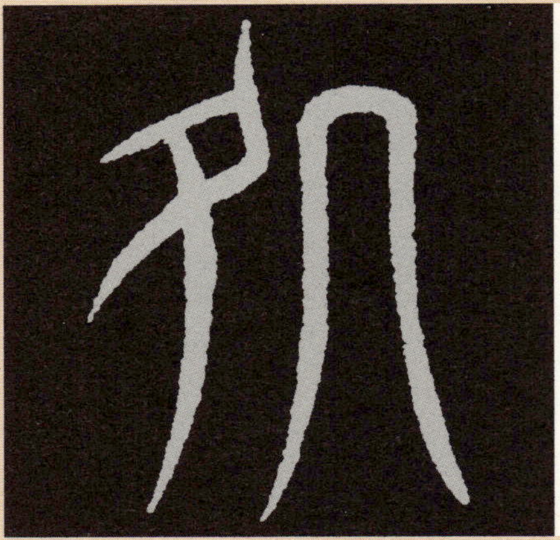

篆书"处"字外形像一个人坐在凳子上休息，意思是停止。

The seal script of "处" resembles a person sitting on the bench. It means stop.

篆书"暑"字是上形下声，由"日"和"者"组成。它的本义是炎热，也指天气炎热的日子。

The seal script of "暑" consists of two characters "日"and "者", with the upper part standing for the meaning and the bottom part standing for the sound. It originally means being extremely hot, and also means the days with extreme heat.

跟着杰瑞写一写

Practicing calligraphy with Jerry

楷书（kai shu）| Regular script

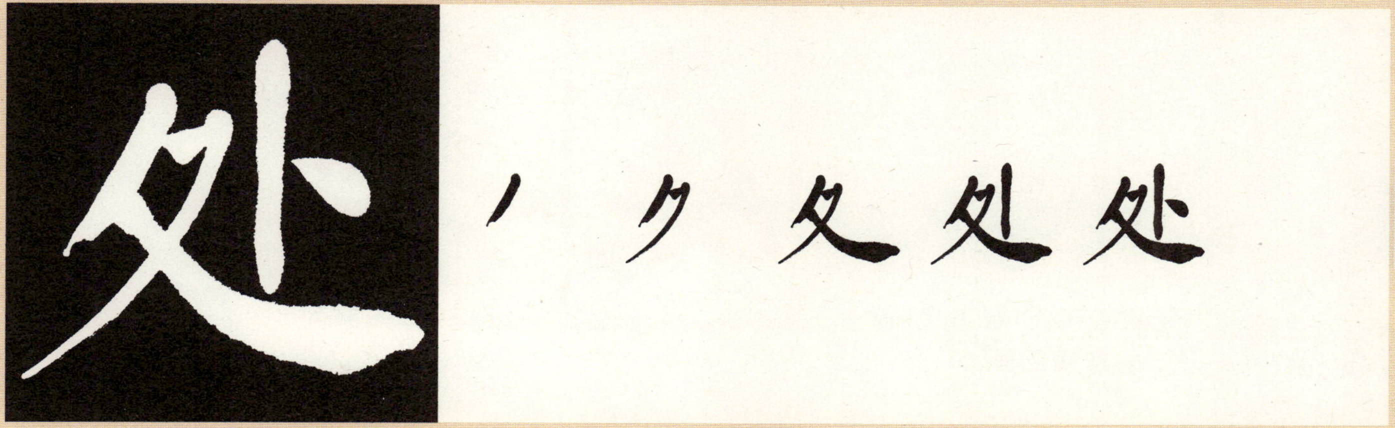

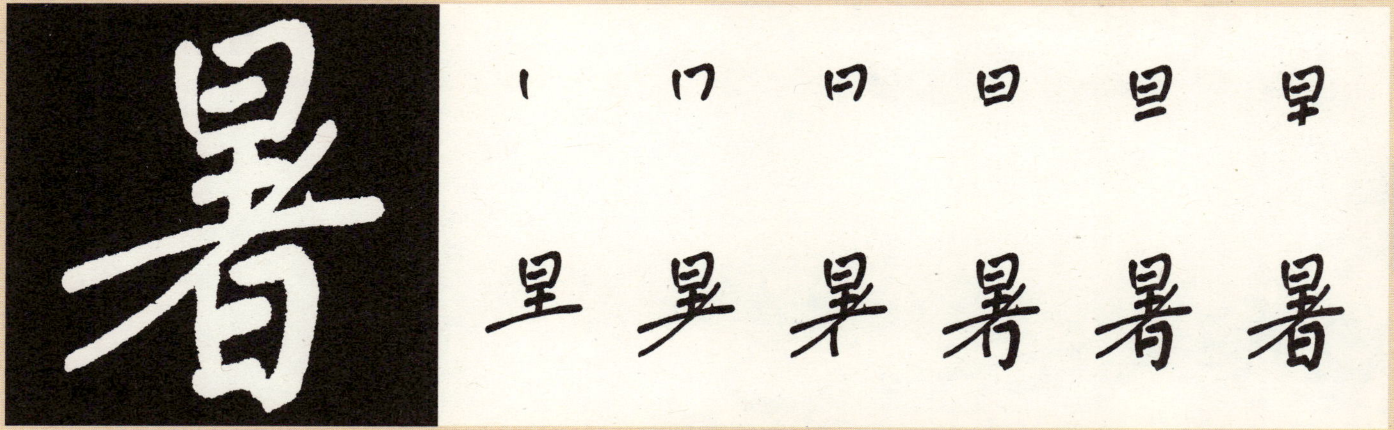

Make a gift with Chinese characters “处暑”

剪剪画画

做处暑的礼物

跟着妮妮和杰瑞做送给朋友的礼物

Let's make some gifts for our friends with Nini and Jerry

剪一剪、画一画

Paper cutting and graphic design

Paper cutting by Nini
妮妮的剪纸

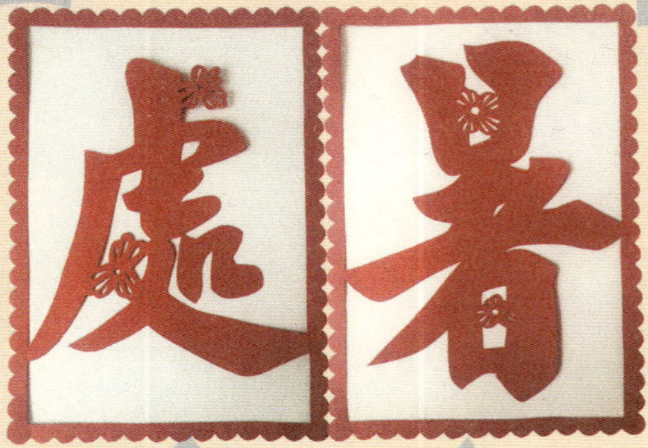

Graphic designed by Jerry
杰瑞的画

猜一猜、说一说

Let's make a guess

Let's make a guess with Nini and Jerry

与妮妮和杰瑞一起猜一猜

与“处暑”对应
的是哪个星座？

Which astrological sign corresponds to End of Heat?

Let's have a competition with Nini and Jerry

与妮妮和杰瑞一起比赛

说出与“处”
有关的词语

Try to say as many words as you can that are relevant to “处”

白露

White Dew

Bai Lu

Important facts about White Dew

The story of **White Dew**

White Dew comes between 7th and 9th September every year. At the time of White Dew, the weather is gradually getting cool; the moisture in the air is condensed into dew on the surface of the ground, grass and trees during night time, so many glittering and crystal-like dewdrops could be found on them early next morning.

Changes after White Dew

The sky is clear and bright with fluffy clouds.
Dewdrops have come into existence.
Swan geese return from the north; swallows migrate to the south.
Walnuts are firm and ripe; it's the time of opening bolls of cotton.

白露的故事

白露大事记

白露的时间点是在每年的9月7～9日之间。白露时节，天气逐渐转凉，夜晚水汽会凝结在地面和草木上，到了第二天的清晨会发现上面有许多晶莹的露珠。

白露变化

天高云淡，露水出现。
鸿雁归来，燕子南飞。
核桃成熟，棉花吐絮。

跟着妮妮学一学
Learning Chinese calligraphy with Nini

篆书 (zhuan shu) | Seal script

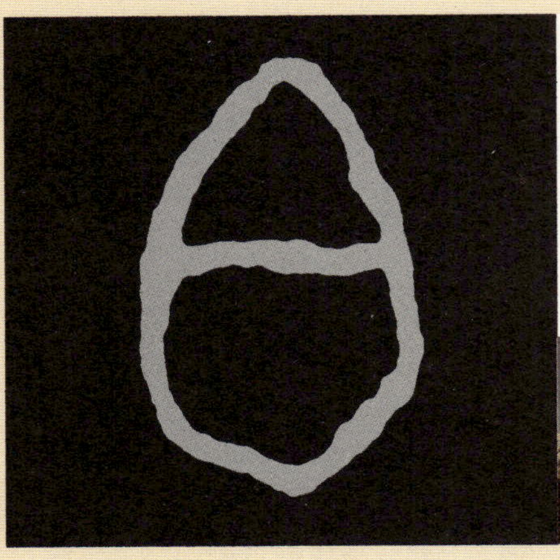

有观点认为，"白"字的甲骨文字形像太阳光线照射的样子。"白"字最初的意思是日光，日光看上去是白色的，所以"白"字多与光亮、白色等含义有关。

A point of view suggests that the oracle script of "白" resembles an image of the sunshine, which initially means sunlight, because the sunlight looks like the white color, so that "白" in most cases, relates to the meaning of brightness and white.

篆书"露"字是上形下声，"雨"是形符，"路"是声符。它的意思是在夜间低温空气中水汽凝结而成的露珠。

The seal script of "露" consists of "雨" and "路". "雨", the upper part stands for the meaning while the bottom part "路" stands for the sound. The whole character represents that the moisture in the air is condensed into dewdrops at the low temperature over the night time.

跟着杰瑞写一写

Practicing calligraphy with Jerry

楷书（kai shu）| Regular script

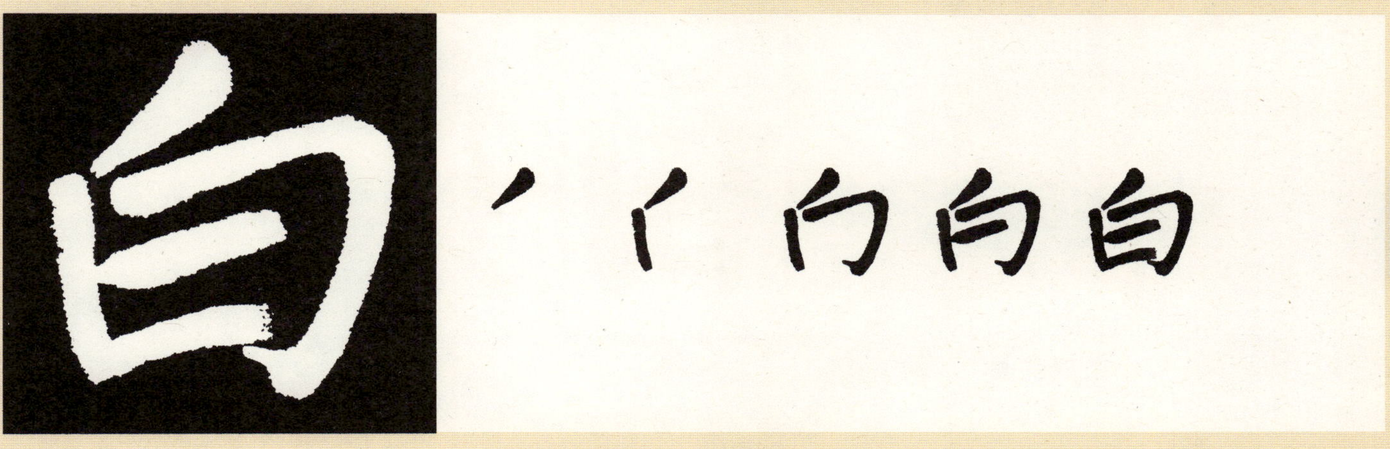

剪一剪、画一画

Paper cutting and graphic design

Make a gift with Chinese characters "白露"

剪剪画画

做白露的礼物

跟着妮妮和杰瑞
做送给朋友的
礼物

Let's make some gifts for our friends with Nini and Jerry

Paper cutting by Nini

妮妮的剪纸

Graphic designed by Jerry

杰瑞的画

猜一猜、说一说

Let's make a guess

Let's make a guess with Nini and Jerry

与妮妮和杰瑞一起猜一猜

与“白露”对应的是哪个星座？

Which astrological sign corresponds to White Dew?

Let's have a competition with Nini and Jerry

与妮妮和杰瑞一起比赛

说出与“白”有关的词语

Try to say as many words as you can that are relevant to “白”

秋分

Autumn Equinox

Qiu Fen

Important facts about Autumn Equinox

The story of
Autumn Equinox

Autumn Equinox comes between 22nd and 24th September every year. On the day of Autumn Equinox, day and night are equally long in both north and south hemispheres again. From Autumn Equinox on, the daytime in north hemisphere starts to get shorter while the night time gets longer. Autumn Equinox marks the arrival of autumn harvest season. People start harvesting rice, sorghum, corn and soybeans, and also making preparations for winter wheat planting.

Changes after Autumn Equinox

Sweet osmanthus are now in full bloom.
A fragrant smell from a variety of fruits is spreading everywhere.
Thunder begins to soften; rain falls less and less.
People appreciate the moon at the Mid-Autumn Festival.
This is also the busiest time in autumn harvest season.

秋分大事记

秋分的故事

秋分的时间点是在每年的9月22～24日之间。在秋分这一天，南北半球的昼夜时间再次相等。从秋分开始，北半球变得日短夜长。秋分标志着秋收时节的到来，水稻、高粱、玉米、大豆开始收割，冬小麦也开始准备播种。

秋分变化

桂花盛开，瓜果飘香。
雷始收声，降水减少。
中秋赏月，秋收大忙。

At the time of Autumn Equinox, it is just happening to get approach to the Mid-Autumn Festival, which is an important Chinese traditional festival. On 15th August of every Chinese lunar year, the moon is full and bright, which symbolizes the family reunion. Therefore the Mid-Autumn Festival is also called the Day of Reunion. Chinese people usually gather together to appreciate the moon and taste mooncakes with their family members, as the celebration of a whole family reunion.

appreciate the moon

taste mooncakes

中秋节

秋分时节恰逢临近中国的重要传统节日中秋节。每年农历八月十五，月亮明亮圆满，象征着家人团圆，因而中秋节又叫团圆节。中秋之夜人们会和家人一起赏月、吃月饼，以此庆祝阖家团圆。

赏月

吃月饼

篆书（zhuan shu）| Seal script

篆书“秋”字的左半部分像一株成熟的水稻，右半部分像长须长足的蟋蟀。蟋蟀在秋天鸣叫，所以“秋”的本义是指百谷成熟、蟋蟀鸣叫的季节。

Looking at the structure of the seal script of “秋”, we can find that the left part resembles a plant of mature rice, and the right part resembles a field cricket with long antennas and long feet. Field crickets usually chirp in autumn, so the original meaning of “秋” refers to the season when all grains and crops become mature and field crickets start chirping loudly.

“分”，切开之意。按图所示，在“刀”部的左右各有一笔，表示执刀将物体切分开。

“分” means to cut open. As is shown in the seal script of “刀”, there is a stroke on both sides, which means to cut something apart.

楷书（kai shu）| Regular script

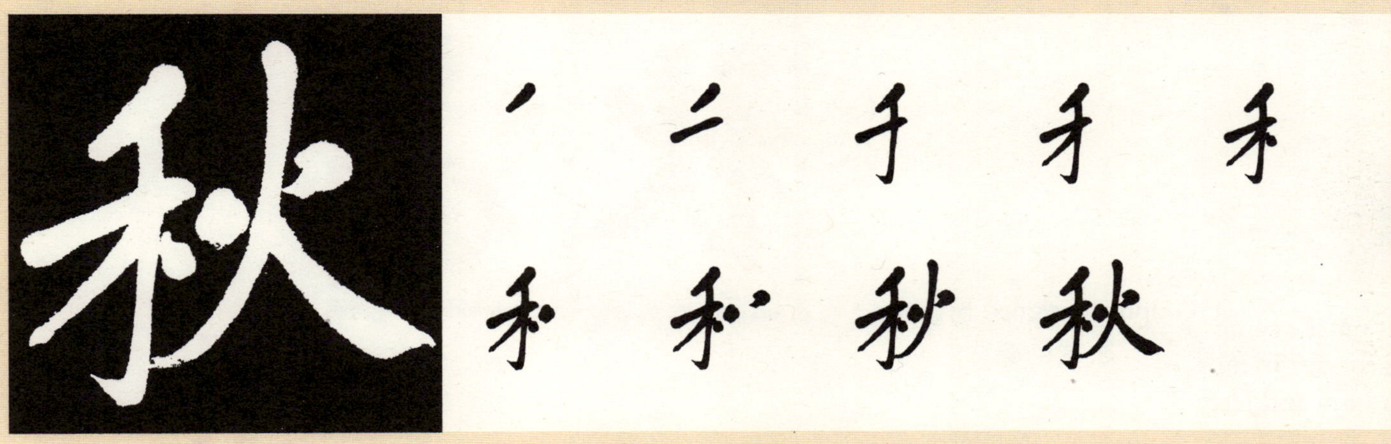

Make a gift with Chinese characters "秋分"

剪剪画画

做秋分的礼物

跟着妮妮和杰瑞做送给朋友的礼物

Let's make some gifts for our friends with Nini and Jerry

剪一剪、画一画

Paper cutting and graphic design

Paper cutting by Nini

妮妮的剪纸

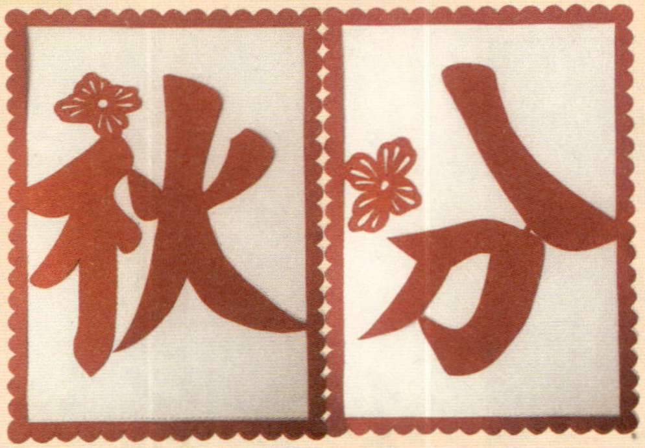

Graphic designed by Jerry

杰瑞的画

猜一猜、说一说

Let's make a guess

Let's make a guess with Nini and Jerry

与妮妮和杰瑞一起猜一猜

与“秋分”对应的是哪个星座？

Which astrological sign corresponds to Autumn Equinox?

Let's have a competition with Nini and Jerry

与妮妮和杰瑞一起比赛

说出与“分”有关的词语

Try to say as many words as you can that are relevant to “分”

寒露

Cold Dew

Han Lu

The story of **Cold Dew**

Important facts about Cold Dew

Cold Dew comes between 8th and 9th October every year. Cold Dew, which means that the temperature has reached a lower level than that in White Dew, the dewdrops on the ground, grass and trees are going to be condensed into frost. At the time of Cold Dew, the weather has changed from cool to cold; it is entering the late autumn time. At the moment, the late rice has started heading and grouting, which is about to enter its maturation period.

Changes after Cold Dew

It is a clear and crisp autumn climate; oranges are ready for picking.
Chrysanthemums are in blossom; maple leaves are just in red.
The guest swan geese have arrived from the north.
People enjoy mountaineering at the Double Ninth Festival.

寒露大事记

寒露的时间点是在每年的10月8～9日之间。寒露的意思是，此时气温已经变得比白露时节更低，地面和草木上的露水已经要凝结成霜了。寒露时节，天气由凉爽向寒冷转变，开始进入深秋季节。这时晚稻开始抽穗灌浆，即将进入成熟期。

寒露变化

秋高气爽，柑橘成熟。
菊花盛开，枫叶正红。
鸿雁来宾，重阳登高。

Every September 9th in Chinese lunar calendar is the Chung-yeung Festival, and this day is also named "the Double Ninth Festival," which is an important Chinese folk traditional festival. On the day of celebrating it, the whole family is outing to appreciate the beautiful autumn view, such as looking far into a distance by climbing mountains, enjoying flourishing chrysanthemums, and tasting the delicious Chung-yeung cakes. Due to the pronunciation of "September 9th" in Chinese lunar calendar and of "longer and longer" sharing the same, which has a moral of long life, the Chung-yeung Festival has been regarded as " Senior's Day". This promotes the tradition on paying respect to the elderly people in Chinese heritage.

looking far into a distance by climbing mountains

enjoying flourishing chrysanthemums

tasting Chung-yeung cakes

重阳节

每年农历的九月初九是重阳节，这一天又被称为"九九重阳"，是中国民间重要的传统节日。在这一天，全家人要一起出游赏秋，登高远眺、观赏菊花、吃重阳糕。由于"九九"与"久久"同音，有长寿的寓意，因此重阳节又被定为"老人节"，弘扬尊老敬老的民族传统。

登高远眺

观赏菊花

吃重阳糕

篆书 (zhuan shu) | Seal script

篆书"寒"字外框表示房屋，下面是冰，字的中间是人在草堆里的样子。整个字表示在冰冷天气人躲进屋子里，钻入草堆中避寒，意思是寒冷。

The outer part of the seal script of "寒" stands for shelter, the bottom part stands for ice and the middle part resembles an image of a man in the rick. The whole character indicates a man who stays in the house and burrows himself into the rick in order to keep away from the coldness under the freezing weather. It means freezing coldness.

篆书"露"字是上形下声，"雨"是形符，"路"是声符。它的意思是在夜间低温空气中水汽凝结而成的露珠。

The seal script of "露" consists of "雨" and "路". "雨", the upper part stands for the meaning while the bottom part "路" stands for the sound. The whole character represents that the moisture in the air is condensed into dewdrops at the low temperature over the night time.

跟着杰瑞写一写

Practicing calligraphy with Jerry

楷书（kai shu）| Regular script

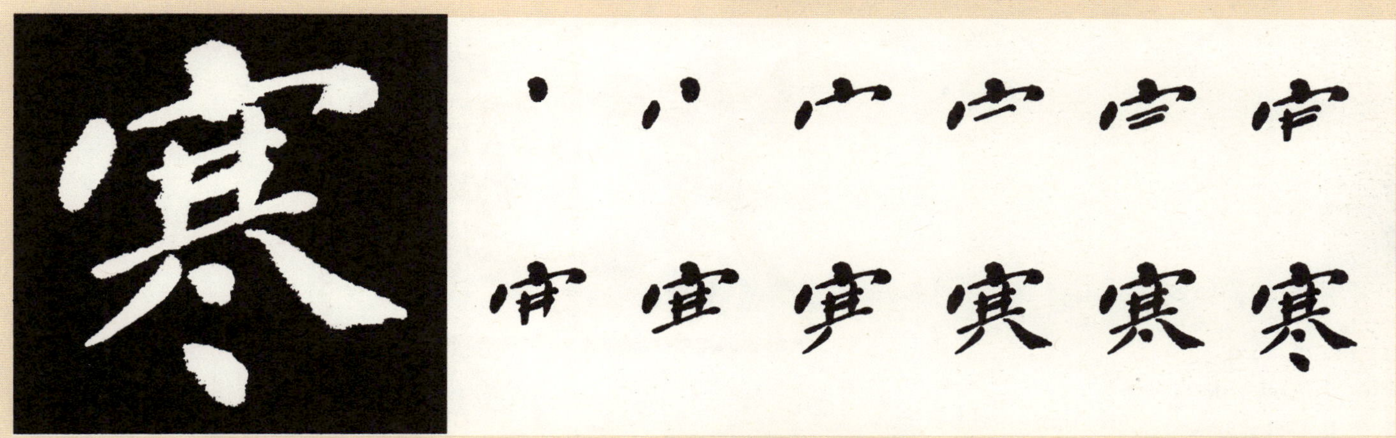

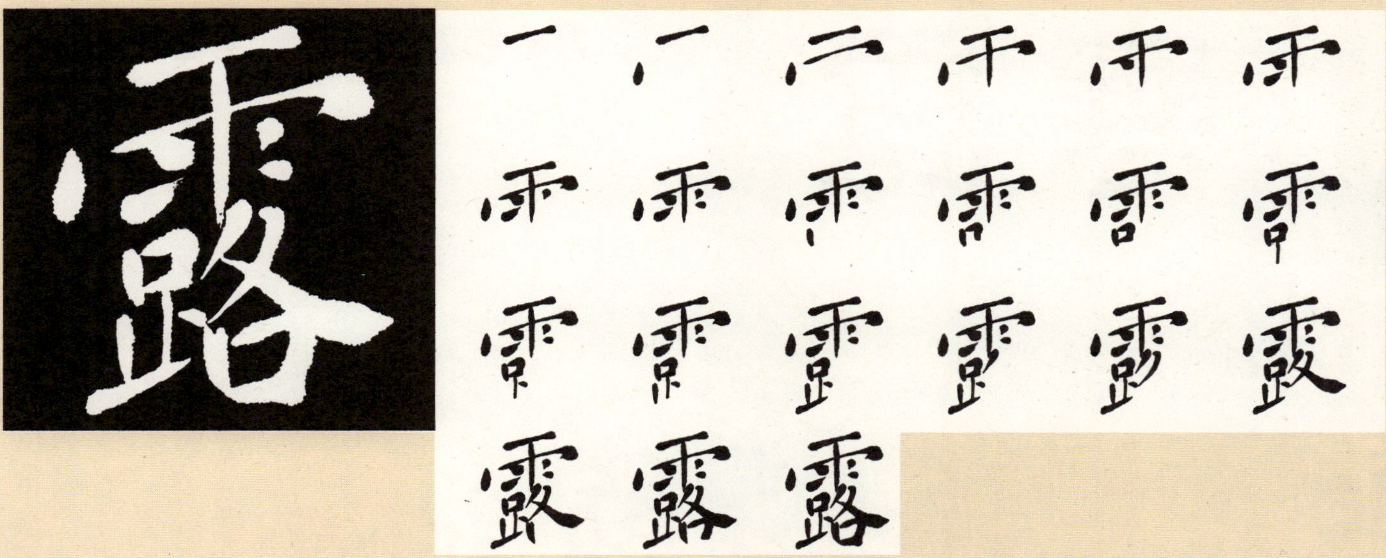

Make a gift with Chinese characters “寒露”

剪剪画画
做寒露的礼物

跟着妮妮和杰瑞
做送给朋友的
礼物

Let’s make some gifts for our friends with Nini and Jerry

剪一剪、画一画

Paper cutting and graphic design

Paper cutting by Nini
妮妮的剪纸

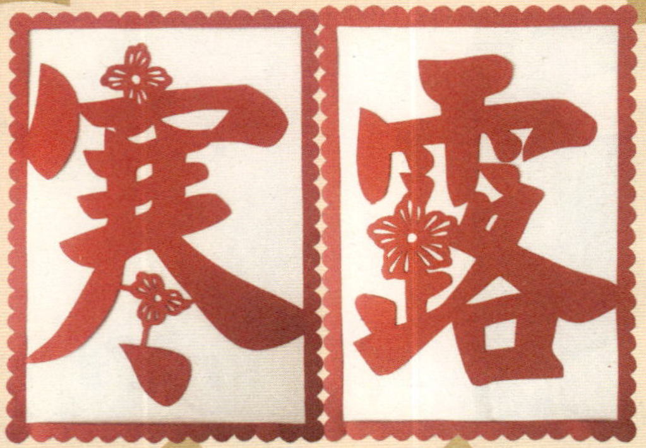

Graphic designed by Jerry
杰瑞的画

猜一猜、说一说

Let's make a guess

Let's make a guess with Nini and Jerry

与妮妮和杰瑞一起猜一猜

与“寒露”对应的是哪个星座？

Which astrological sign corresponds to Cold Dew?

Let's have a competition with Nini and Jerry

与妮妮和杰瑞一起比赛

说出与“露”有关的词语

Try to say as many words as you can that are relevant to “露”

霜降

First Frost
Shuang Jiang

The story of **First Frost**

Important facts about First Frost

First Frost comes between 23rd and 24th October every year. The arrival of First Frost marks that autumn has drawn to a close, and the weather becomes colder and colder. At the time of First Frost, if the temperature at nighttime drops below zero degree, the moisture in the air is condensed and thin frost is formed on the surface of the ground or plants. Meanwhile, it is time to start reaping the late rice. Until now, the peak busy farming in the autumn harvest season is basically over.

Changes after First Frost

Frost appears and the temperature begins to descend.

It is a harvest season for the late rice.

Hibiscuses come to blossom; persimmons are ready for picking.

Grass and trees become withered and tree leaves are falling down.

Many animals start hibernating.

霜降大事记

霜降的时间点是每年的10月23～24日之间。霜降的到来标志着秋季已经进入尾声，天气变得越来越寒冷。霜降时节，夜晚的温度如果下降到零度以下，空气中的水蒸汽就会在地面或者植物表面凝结，形成细小的冰霜。此时晚稻开始收割，秋收农忙基本结束。

霜降变化

初霜始现，晚稻收割。
芙蓉花开，柿子成熟。
草木黄落，动物冬眠。

跟着妮妮学一学
Learning Chinese calligraphy with Nini

篆书 (zhuan shu) | Seal script

篆书"霜"字是上形下声，"雨"是形符，"相"是声符。它的意思是秋冬时节在低温中凝结的、杀伤植物的水汽结晶。

The seal script of "霜" consists of "雨" and "相". "雨", the upper part stands for the meaning while the bottom part "相" stands for the sound. It means the frost, which is condensed by the moisture in the air at a low temperature in late autumn and winter time. Frost does harm to the growth of plants.

篆书"降"字的左边部分表示盘山石阶，右边部分表示两足，足趾向下。整个字的意思是人从高处往下走。

Looking at the seal script of "降", we can find that the left part stands for mountain steps, and the right part stands for two feet, with toes pointing downwards. The whole character means that a person is walking downwards from an upper level.

霜

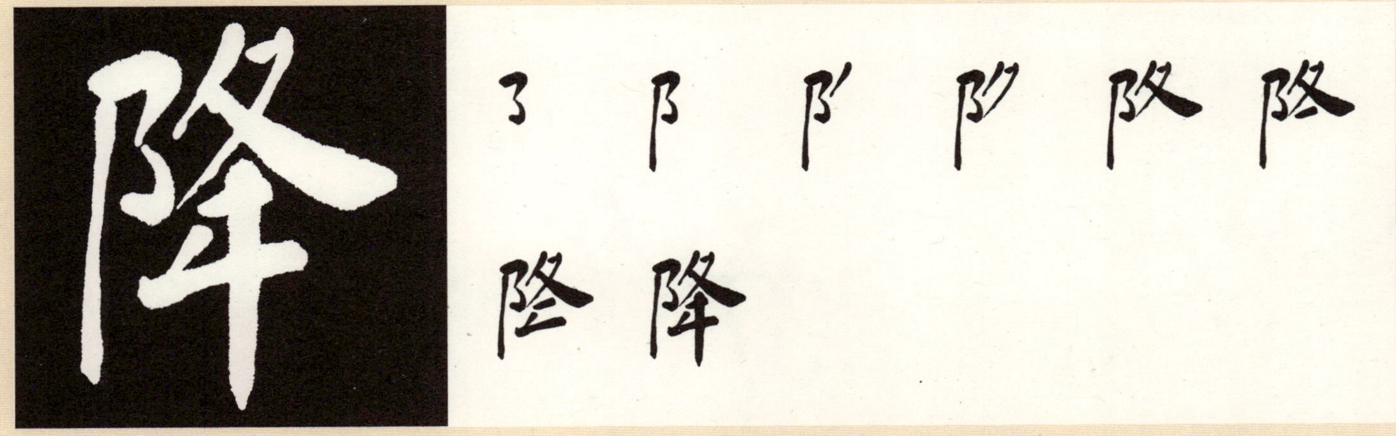
降

Make a gift with Chinese characters “霜降”

剪剪画画 做霜降的礼物

跟着妮妮和杰瑞做送给朋友的礼物

Let’s make some gifts for our friends with Nini and Jerry

剪一剪、画一画

Paper cutting and graphic design

Paper cutting by Nini

妮妮的剪纸

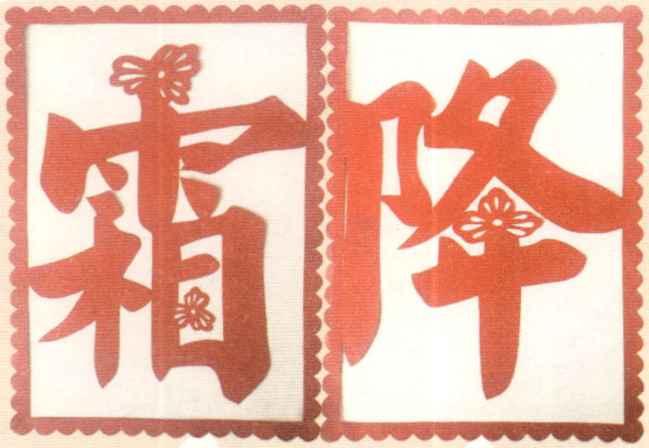

Graphic designed by Jerry

杰瑞的画

猜一猜、说一说

Let's make a guess

Let's make a guess with Nini and Jerry

与妮妮和杰瑞一起猜一猜

与"霜降"对应的是哪个星座？

Which astrological sign corresponds to First Frost?

Let's have a competition with Nini and Jerry

与妮妮和杰瑞一起比赛

说出与"降"有关的词语

Try to say as many words as you can that are relevant to "降"

后记

自2014年完成了“书法小联合国”文化特色教材《十二生肖我来写》之后，一直收到不同国家各级学校老师发来的邮件，询问是否可以买到课程的示范录像，也有老师与家长鼓励我继续编写一些有趣的关于中国传统文化的书法教材。

编写海外书法文化启蒙教材是一件十分艰难的事，看起来只是一本几十页的小书，要编写好绝非一日之功。首先要找到一个好的素材，之后要在不同的文化语境中反复进行教学实验，咨询各方专家的意见，最后方能定稿。多年来，“书法小联合国”国际系列教材编写的目标是：教材既要遵循受众国的文化习俗，又要在编写上做到准确、有趣，把中国故事讲好。

《风调雨顺：春夏秋冬》四册书法文化启蒙教材从酝酿到动笔撰写就花了近五年的时间，教材主要实验地在北美与南美部分学校，实验教材在使用过程中受到学生与教师的欢迎。该教材一方面介绍中国古代气象文化，以故事主人公中国妮妮给美国杰瑞讲故事的方式展开情节；另一方面，通过讲解汉字的构字特点来帮助不同文化背景的学生认知汉字里的文化，并采用二维码形式附上书法教学视频，方便实用，帮助学习者在书法、绘画、剪纸等艺术形式中加强对中国文化的整体理解。

感谢前联合国秘书长潘基文先生、上海交通大学张伟民教授、美国理海大学康妮教授、纽约大学唐力行教授、联合国国际学校孙青倩等老师在该教材编写过程中提出的中肯建议。感谢华东师范大学出版社王焰社长在教材出版过程中的大力支持。相信这四册“书法小联合国”汉字书法文化系列教材的顺利出版，会在中国书法文化国际教材开发中发挥积极的示范作用。

周斌于中国书法文化国际传播研究所

2017年10月28日

Postscript

Since the publication of *Let Me Write the Twelve Zodiac Signs* which belongs to the special course on calligraphy culture by United Association of Calligraphy in 2014, I have been receiving mails from parents and teachers from different schools all over the world. They asked me whether they could buy the video recordings of some demo lessons. And some of them encouraged me to keep writing more interesting calligraphy course books relevant to traditional Chinese culture.

It is not an easy task to compile a course book on calligraphy culture for overseas learners. Just as Rome was not built in a day, such a thin book of tens of pages also cannot be completed within a day. First of all, we need to find a suitable topic and its relevant materials. Then, we need to test the course book through continuous classroom instructions in various cultural contexts. After that we consult experts from all walks of life, and with feedback from classrooms, we finally make the decision to mass produce the course book. Our international course book series aim not only to suit the customs of the overseas learners but also to tell the stories of Chinese culture with accuracy and amusement.

From the blueprint to the first draft of the four course books — *Spring/Summer/Fall/Winter: Season with Timely Breeze and Rain for Crop Raising* — for the enlightenment on Chinese calligraphy culture, it took us nearly five years to present them to the public. These course books were put on trial mainly in some schools in North and South America and got very positive feedback from both teachers and students. This course book series introduces Chinese people's understanding of the climate in ancient time through stories told by a Chinese character named Nini to an American character named Jerry. Furthermore, we have selected some ancient Chinese characters to help students from different cultural backgrounds get a better appreciation of the culture of Chinese characters. Moreover, we have attached a QR code in the part Practicing Calligraphy with Jerry. If you scan the QR code, you can watch videos teaching you how to write the characters. Learners' comprehensive understanding of Chinese culture will be improved by learning and practicing Chinese calligraphy.

Here I want to extend my sincere gratitude to the former UN Secretary-General, Mr Ban Ki-moon; Professor Zhang Weimin from Shanghai Jiao Tong University, Professor Connie from Lehigh University, and Professor Lixing Tang from New York University for their pertinent suggestions during the process of compiling these course books. I'm also grateful to president of East China Normal University Press, Mrs Yan Wang, for her substantial support during the publication process. I firmly believe that the publication of these four course books would play a very positive role in the development of international course books on Chinese calligraphy culture.

Zhou Bin

In Chinese Calligraphy Culture Education and Communication Center

28th October 2017

图书在版编目（CIP）数据

风调雨顺. 秋 / 周斌，周佳楠主编. —上海：华东师范大学出版社，2018
ISBN 978-7-5675-7958-3

Ⅰ. ①风… Ⅱ. ①周… ②周… Ⅲ. ①汉语 - 对外汉语教学 - 语言读物 Ⅳ. ① H195.5

中国版本图书馆 CIP 数据核字（2018）第 147041 号

风调雨顺 · 秋

主　　编　周　斌　周佳楠
策划编辑　王　焰
责任编辑　曹　琛
特约审读　曹一凡
责任校对　张多多
封面设计　刘怡霖

出版发行　华东师范大学出版社
社　　址　上海市中山北路 3663 号 邮编 200062
网　　址　www.ecnupress.com.cn
电　　话　021-60821666　行政传真　021-62572105
客服电话　021-62865537　门市（邮购）电话　021-62869887
地　　址　上海市中山北路 3663 号华东师范大学校内先锋路口
网　　店　http://hdsdcbs.tmall.com

印 刷 者　上海盛通时代印刷有限公司
开　　本　700 × 1000　12 开
印　　张　7⅓
字　　数　52 千字
版　　次　2018 年 8 月第一版
印　　次　2018 年 8 月第一次
书　　号　ISBN 978-7-5675-7958-3/G · 11273
定　　价　48.00 元
出 版 人　王　焰

练习册使用说明

本书为《风调雨顺 · 秋》教材的配套练习册，希望通过二十四节气相关汉字的书法练习，使读者掌握书法学习的要领。本练习册通过对汉字字体笔顺和笔画的分析，为学习者掌握汉字的书写方法提供指导。同时，描红及空格练习也便于读者对照示范汉字进行反复书写。

This is the workbook for our course book *Fall: Season with Timely Breeze and Rain for Crop Raising*. We hope that readers will be able to master the principles of writing Chinese calligraphy after practicing the Chinese characters relevant to the Twenty-four Solar Terms. This workbook is going to give a detailed demonstration on strokes and the organization of these strokes in our sample characters, so as to provide a guidance of writing Chinese calligraphy for our learners. At the same time, the particular framework we offer in this workbook for learners to write in is very helpful because learners can practice repeatedly by imitating.

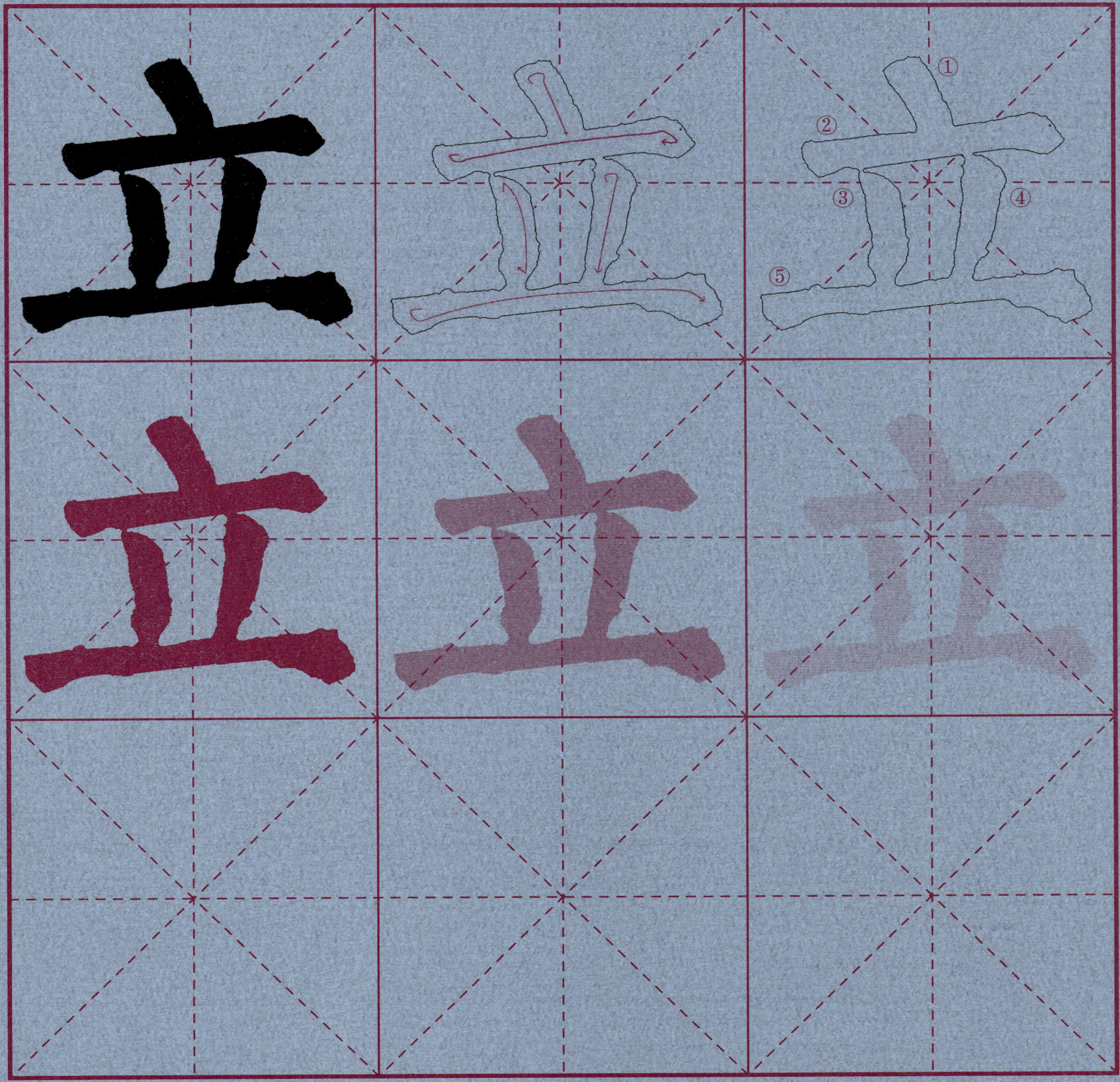
立
①
②
③
④
⑤

秋 秋 秋

秋 秋 秋

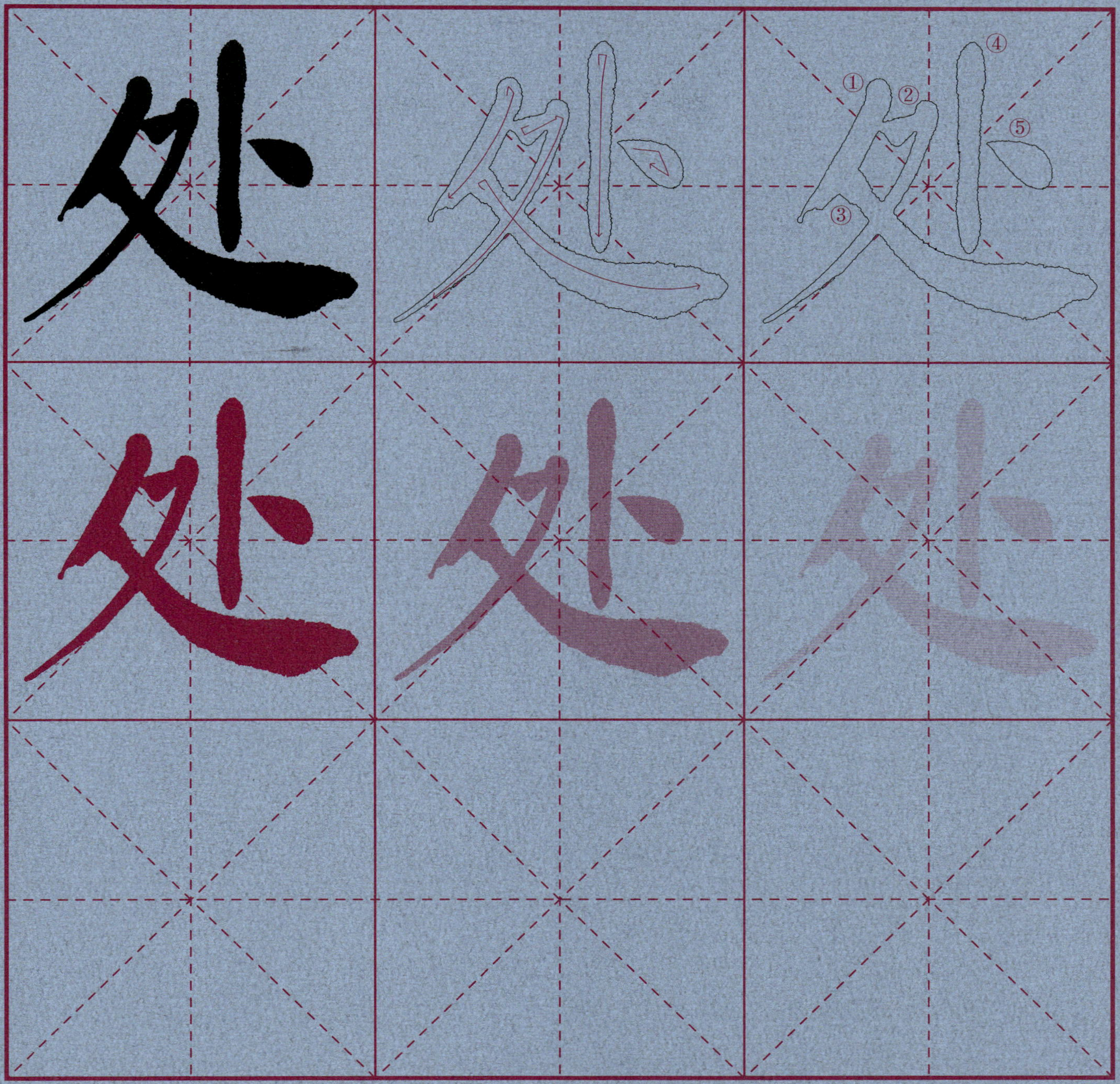
处
①
②
③
④
⑤

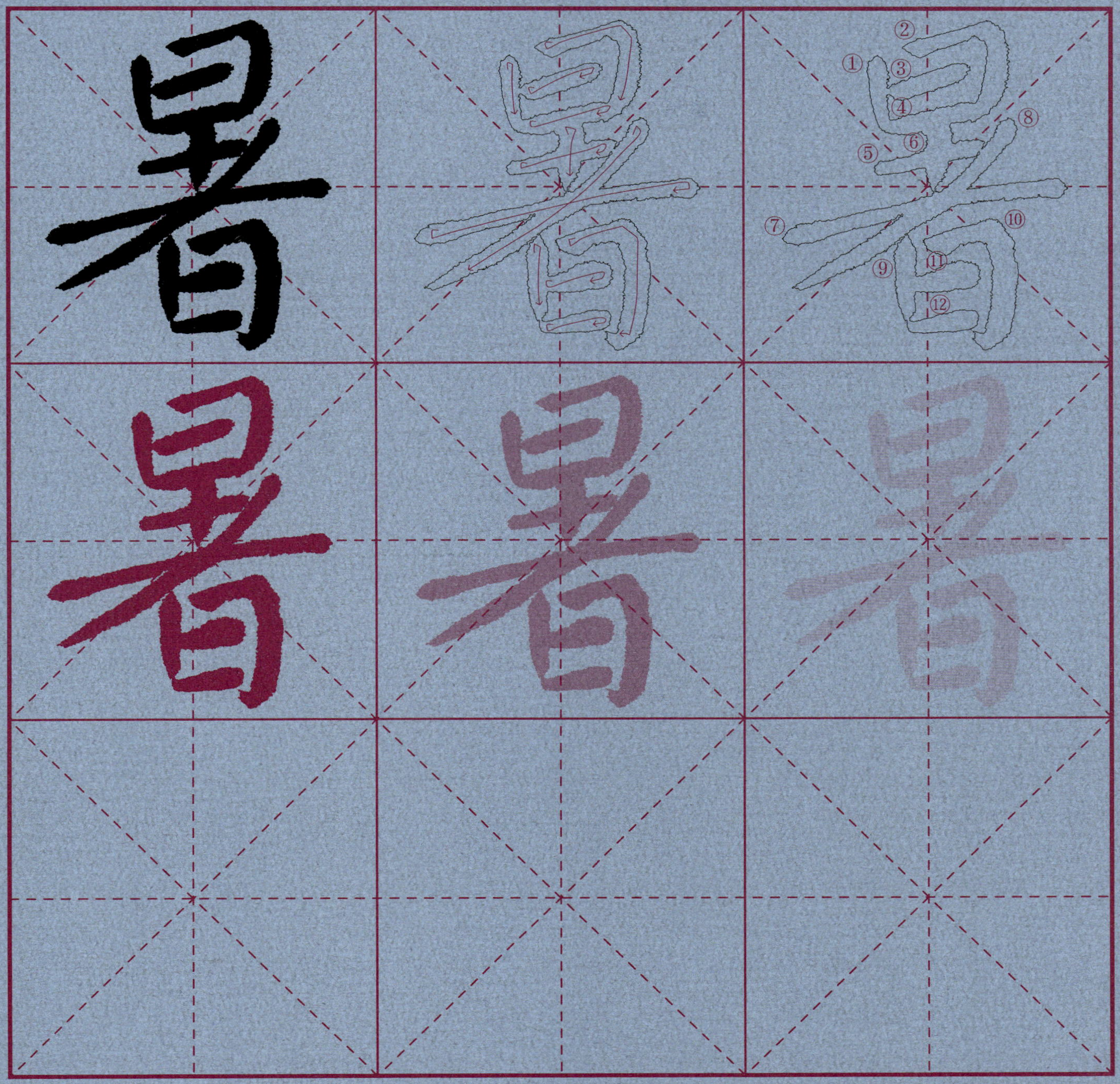
暑 暑 暑
暑 暑 暑

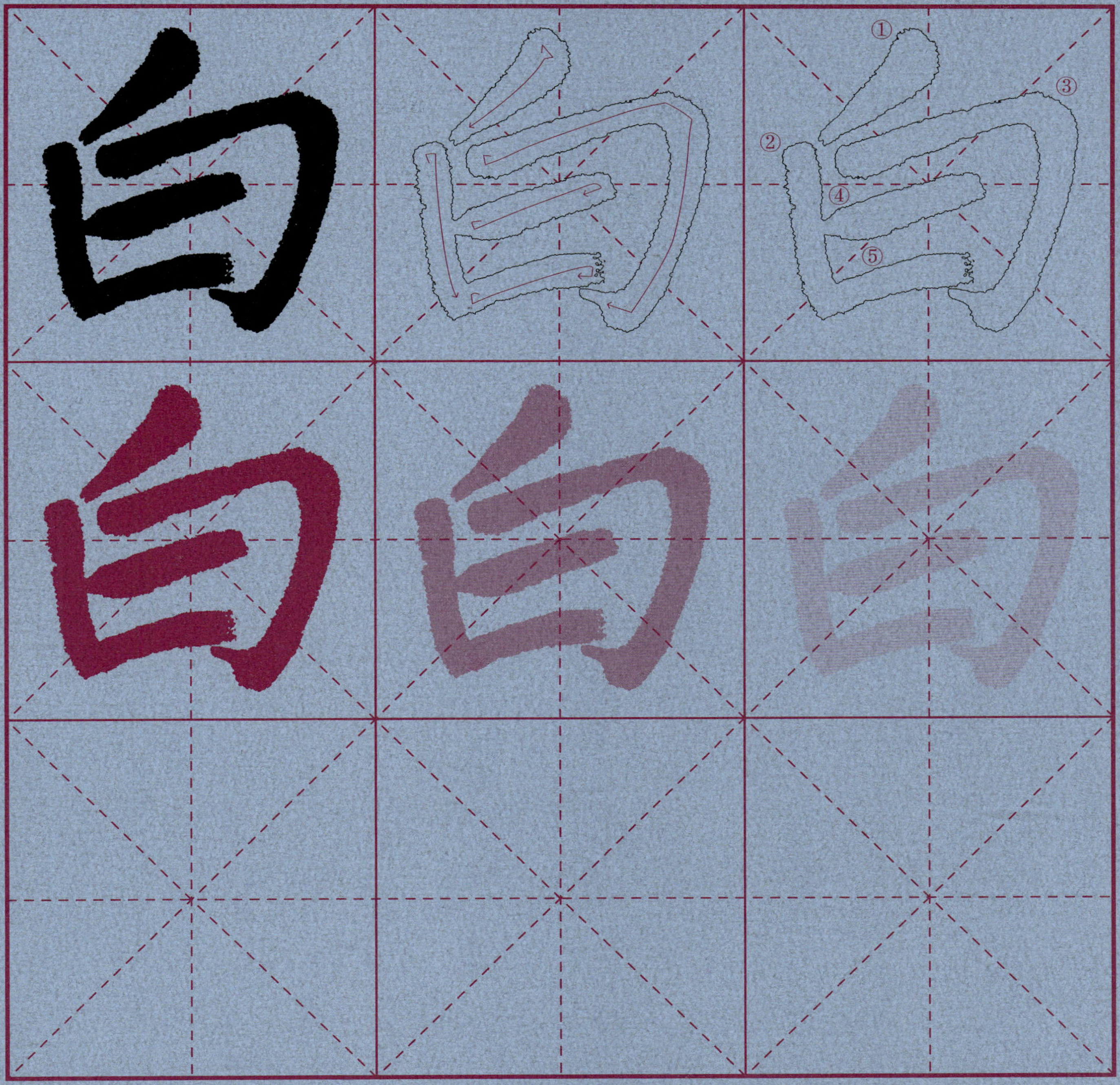
白
①
②
③
④
⑤

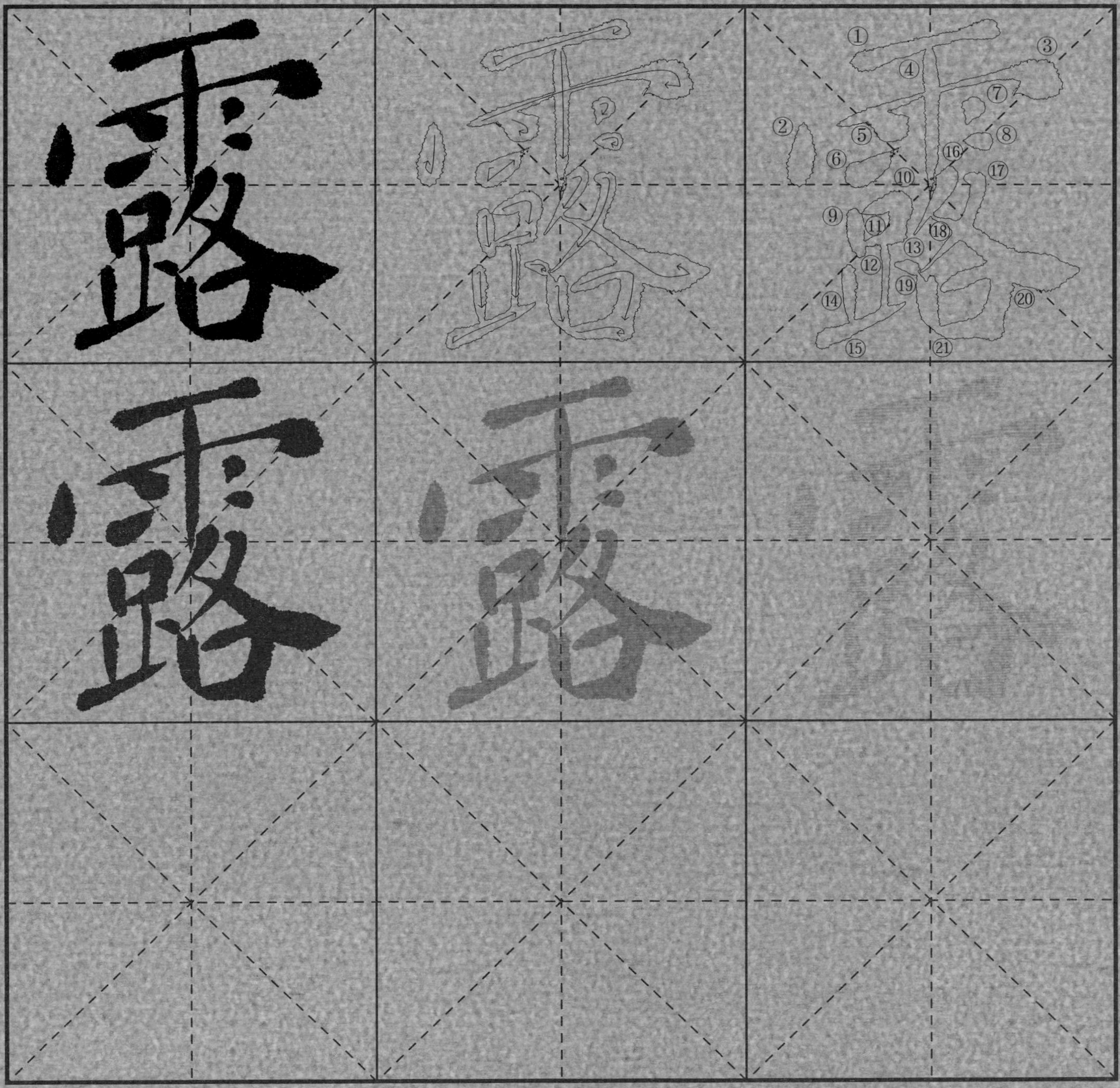
露

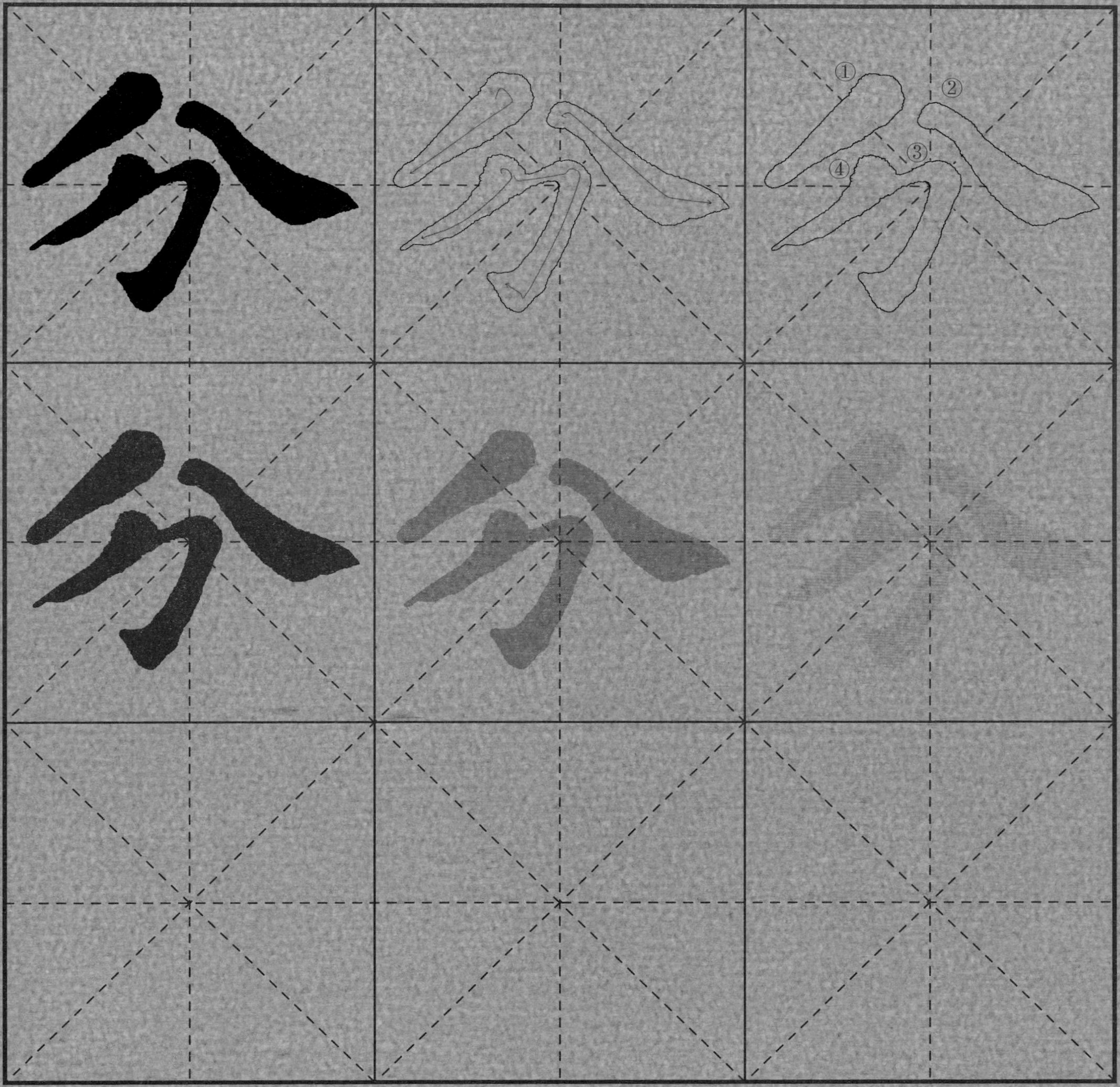
分
① ② ③ ④

寒

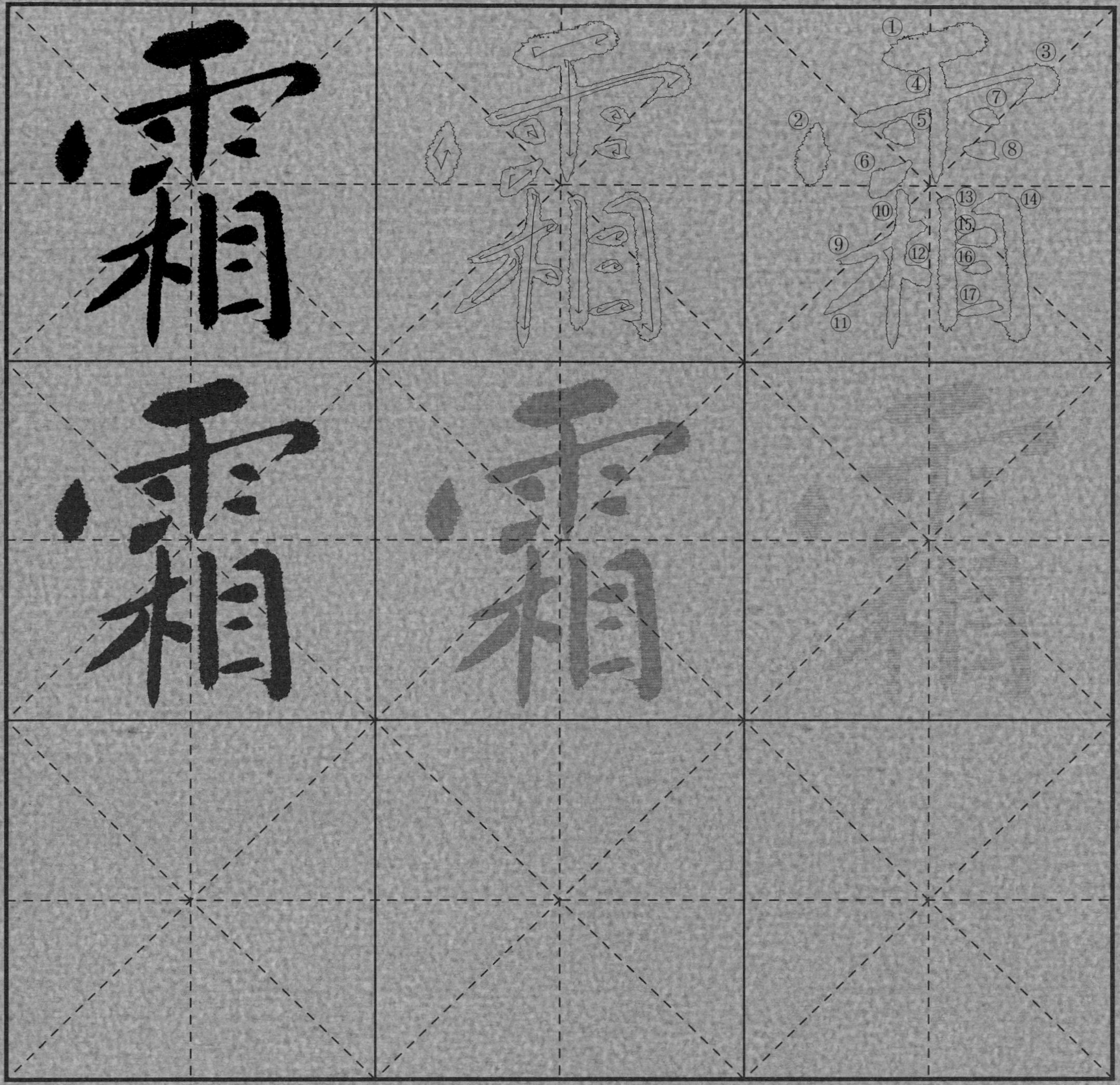
霜

降 降 降
① ② ③ ④ ⑤ ⑥ ⑦ ⑧
降 降 降